D1315915

NUCLEAR WARFARE

Modern Military Techniques

Aircraft Carriers
Military Helicopters
Bombers
Amphibious Techniques
Tanks
Artillery
Fighters
Submarines

MODERN MILITARY TECHNIQUES
NUCLEAR WARFARE

Laurence W. Martin

Illustrations by
Tony Gibbons, Peter Sarson, and Tony Bryan

Lerner Publications Company • Minneapolis

Library of Congress Cataloging-in-Publication Data
Martin, Laurence W.
  Nuclear warfare/Laurence Martin; illustrations by Tony Gibbons,
Peter Sarson, Tony Bryan.
      p.   cm. — (Modern military techniques)
  Includes index.
  Summary: Discusses the origin, spread, and main types of nuclear
weapons, humanity's attempts to control them, the possible
developments and aftermath of nuclear warfare, and the nuclear
disarmament movement.
  ISBN 0-8225-1384-6 (lib. bdg.)
  1. Nuclear warfare—Juvenile literature. 2. Nuclear disarmament—
Juvenile literature. |1. Nuclear warfare. 2. Nuclear
disarmament.| I. Gibbons, Tony, ill. II. Sarson, Peter, ill.
III. Bryan, Tony, ill. IV. Title. V. Series.
U263.M333   1988   87-36068
355.′0217—dc19   CIP
                                           AC

Manufactured in the United States of America

1 2 3 4 5 6 7 8 9 10 97 96 95 94 93 92 91 90 89 88

CONTENTS

1 The Origin and Spread of Nuclear Weapons

The Nature of the Nuclear Revolution

The discovery that it is possible to release the energy within the atomic structure of certain elements has led to the manufacture of weapons of unprecedented destructiveness. Such weapons present a great danger as they are capable of causing damage on an immense scale and possibly killing hundreds of millions of people while destroying the basis of civilized life over wide areas.

Even when applied to such peaceful uses as generating electrical power the release of nuclear energy causes serious hazards and safety problems. But technology alone does not pose the threat of nuclear war. This danger exists only when people band together to fight each other. Wars have been waged for thousands of years, and for thousands of years people have tried to win by using the most powerful weapons available.

In the 19th century, the rapid advance of modern technology and industrial organization greatly increased both the destructive power of armed forces and the capacity of societies both to resist and to recover from an attack. In the present century, these advances have already resulted in two massively destructive world wars, causing so much damage and upheaval that the post-war world bore little resemblance to the aims for which either side had gone to war. These experiences led many to question whether modern war on a large scale remained a practical – let alone a morally justifiable – way to achieve political purposes.

Nuclear weapons, as we shall see, carry the possibilities of destruction to a new level, and they are able to inflict far greater damage within a few hours than previously resulted from years of warfare. This not only makes the consequences of war worse but also raises new concerns about controlling such a destructive process. Fearing the consequences of losing control, the nations possessing nuclear weapons have, therefore, become extremely cautious in managing these dangers and in their dealing with each other. Indeed, nuclear weapons have not been used in war since the first two atomic bombs were dropped on Japan in 1945. And although wars continue to be frequent in the so-called *Third World countries*, and the *nuclear powers* – countries possessing nuclear weapons – have sometimes participated in them, there have been no wars between the two blocks of economically advanced nations that are grouped around the two greatest nuclear powers, the Soviet Union and the United States of America.

The Theory of Nuclear Deterrence

Over the past few decades, ways of living with nuclear weapons have evolved, creating political systems that everyone hopes will prevent such weapons from ever being used. The main feature of these systems is *nuclear deterrence*. Quite soon after nuclear weapons were developed, the difficulty of creating an effective defense against a nuclear attack made some experts decide that *active defense*, such as shooting down bombers, was impossible and that *passive defense* – building air raid shelters, evacuating people, etc. – would not do much good either. Safety could only come from persuading potential attackers not to attack at all, and this could best be done by convincing them that they would suffer an equally bad attack in return. This threat of *retaliation*, therefore, would perhaps serve to deter the possible aggressor.

While deterrence is not a new idea in the nuclear age, what is new about nuclear deterrence is, first, that it may be the only defense possible and, secondly, that a well-designed nuclear force could create retaliatory threats so great that no leader would ever act to bring about such destruction

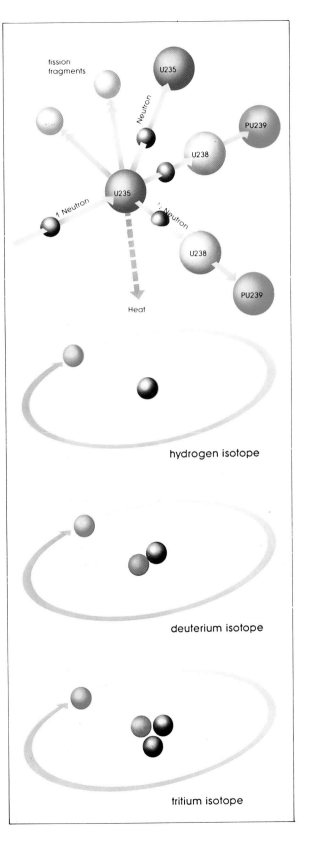

Right: Atoms are composed of a nucleus containing protons and neutrons that is surrounded by a varying number of electrons. In a *chemical reaction*, the electrons are rearranged, but the protons and neutrons in the nucleus are rearranged during a *nuclear reaction*. If very heavy atoms with many protons and neutrons are bombarded by neutrons, they may split and release further neutrons to continue the *chain reaction*. The only natural element that can sustain such a reaction is uranium U235, which has 92 protons and 143 neutrons. An artificial element, plutonium (Pu239), can be made by bombarding the common uranium U238, and this, too, can sustain a chain reaction.

To achieve these fission reactions explosively requires assembling a dense *supercritical mass* of *fissionable* material by compressing it with a high explosive trigger.

Below right: The other way to release the immense energy of the atom is to submit the light nuclei of hydrogen to the high temperatures created by a fission explosion. Such a fusion trigger can make the atoms of hydrogen *fuse*, or join together.

Large amounts of fissionable material might begin a chain reaction spontaneously, which limits the *yield*, or explosive power, of fission weapons. *Fusion*, or thermonuclear weapons, in contrast, can be made to almost any size because hydrogen will not fuse spontaneously.

deliberately. Consequently, whatever its other military policies, each of the nuclear powers has tried to develop a nuclear retaliatory force that could – even if its enemies struck first – deliver in a *second strike* a blow that would result in unacceptable damage to the aggressor. While not all of the nations possessing such forces necessarily plan to use them to kill as many of the enemy population as possible, large casualties would be an inevitable result of any such attack and *counterattack*.

It can be argued, therefore, that nuclear deterrence has worked because no nuclear weapons have been used since 1945 and no nuclear power has gone to war with another. There is, however, no way of proving this has resulted from nuclear deterrence or that such a fortunate state of affairs will continue.

Indeed, a world of nuclear deterrence has several obvious drawbacks:

1 Because nuclear weapons continue to exist, there is the permanent danger of catastrophe, and the system might produce catastrophe rather than stalemate.

2 The system requires that nuclear powers regard each other as possible enemies, keep calculating military balances against each other, and watch nervously for signs that others have found ways to break the stalemate in their favor and engage in nuclear blackmail, or even an attack.

3 While, theoretically, deterrence could be maintained by only a few nuclear weapons, the kind of suspicion and uncertainty that exists tends to drive nuclear powers to heavy expenditures in order to increase or improve their arsenals. This, in turn, reinforces mutual suspicion.

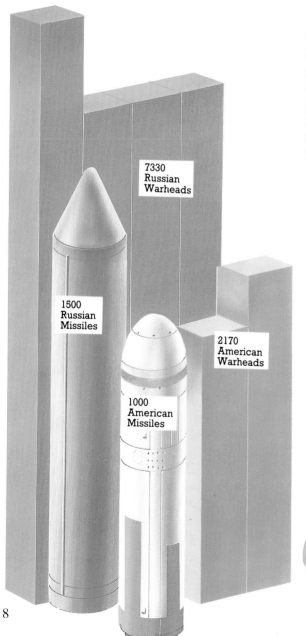

7330
Russian
Warheads

1500
Russian
Missiles

2170
American
Warheads

1000
American
Missiles

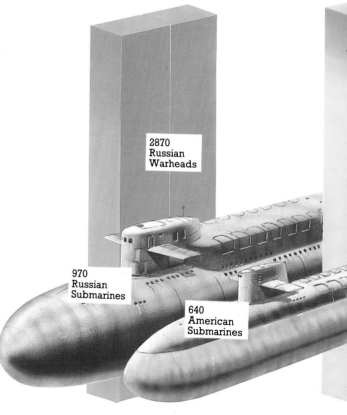

2870
Russian
Warheads

970
Russian
Submarines

640
American
Submarines

4 As such suspicions illustrate, simple nuclear deterrence is based on the assumption that there is no adequate defense yet. In recent years, however, this assumption has been undermined in two ways. First, ways of intercepting bombers and missiles have been much improved. Although any adequate defense against a large-scale nuclear attack in the near future – or, perhaps, ever – seems unlikely, would-be deterrers have to worry about possible defense against their retaliation. This, however, can increase suspicion and competition. Secondly, missiles have become more accurate. While early intercontinental missiles typically missed targets by a mile or two, they can now achieve accuracies of a few hundred feet and will soon be able to arrive within a few yards. Therefore, it might be possible to seek defense by destroying an enemy's retaliatory force before it could be used. The possibility of such a *counterforce strike* against enemy forces rather than against cities or industry could be combined with active defenses against the weakened surviving retaliatory force.

For all of these reasons, deterrence cannot be assured simply by possessing a few nuclear weapons. The weapons also have to be effective against an aggressor's range of *countermeasures*. Such a situation creates an arms competition that would be expensive at best and, at worst, might produce tensions and uncertainties that could lead a nuclear power to believe that attacking was the only way to avert or minimize an attack on itself.

Further difficulties arise from the fact that while the Soviet-United States relationship dominates the nuclear scene, they are not the only nuclear powers. The theory of deterrence is a two-sided, or *bipolar*, concept, and as the number of nuclear powers increases, the possible interrelationships and ways of breaking down will multiply. Moreover, while the term nuclear power is used to describe countries that have nuclear weapons, there are literally dozens of other countries with enough knowledge to make nuclear weapons. Therefore, the theory and practice of deterrence – like that of *disarmament*, or reducing or limiting arms – has to cope with a world of potentially many nuclear-armed nations.

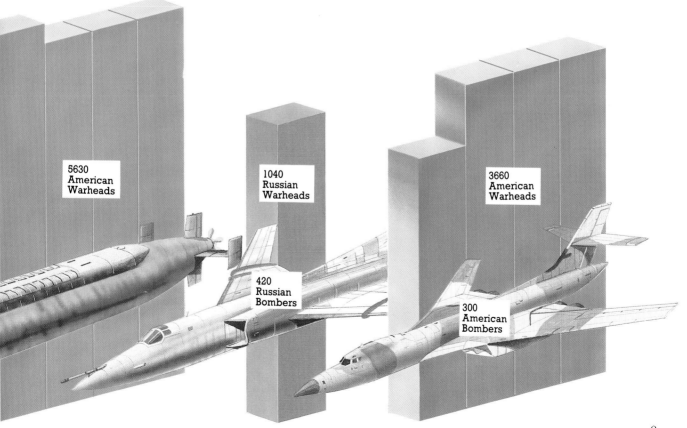

5630
American
Warheads

1040
Russian
Warheads

3660
American
Warheads

420
Russian
Bombers

300
American
Bombers

The Balance of Nuclear Weapons Today

The world now includes five nations that are known to have nuclear weapons: the Soviet Union, the United States, China, France, and the United Kingdom. Israel is widely believed to have manufactured nuclear weapons, and India has detonated a nuclear explosive device that it claims is part of a program to develop peaceful uses for nuclear energy. The forces of the two Superpowers, the U.S.S.R. and the U.S.A., are overwhelmingly the most powerful.

Traditionally, there have been three main ways of launching nuclear weapons: by ballistic missiles, by ballistic missile submarines, and by aircraft. These categories are becoming blurred, however, by such recent innovations as the cruise missile.

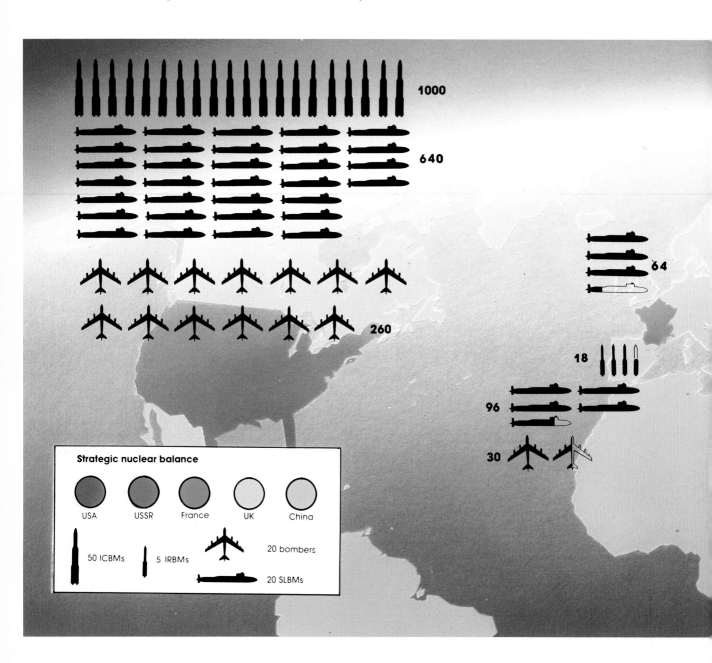

Strategic nuclear balance

USA   USSR   France   UK   China

50 ICBMs   5 IRBMs   20 bombers   20 SLBMs

1000
640
260
64
18
96
30

The map indicates the approximate number of missiles and bombers at the disposal of the nuclear powers. This relatively crude measurement of nuclear power gives a rough idea of relative strength, and it has been much used in arms control negotiations. In practice, many variables determine the effectiveness of a nuclear force, including the number and power of warheads on weapons and the accuracy of delivery. Whether a force is adequate depends also on what it is intended to do, who its enemies are, and how well prepared they are for defense or for retaliation. It is important to notice, for example, that what may look like a large Chinese missile force is almost entirely composed of so-called *intermediate-range missiles*. The Superpowers also have weapons of this range, but they do not normally count them in their *strategic forces*. Nevertheless, by threatening considerable damage to the Soviet Union, these weapons may serve a useful deterrent purpose for China.

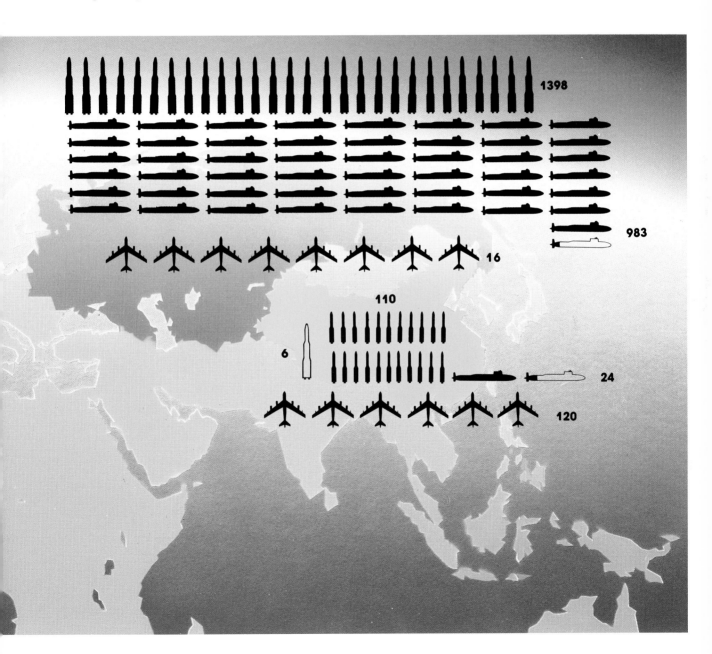

2 The Main Types of Nuclear Weapons

The Ranges of Weapons

Since 1945 when the only two nuclear weapons ever used in war were dropped on Japan, the size, variety, and number of nuclear weapons have multiplied many times. Because of their great destructive potential and relative scarcity, nuclear weapons were originally seen as a means for long-range bombing of industrial and urban targets, or so-called *strategic bombing*. Even though the early bombs were powerful – the Hiroshima-Nagasaki weapons had an explosive force equal to about 15,000 tons of TNT – they still had a fairly restricted effect and were difficult to deliver at long range with great accuracy.

In addition to *free-falling bombs*, there are now two main types of missile. *Ballistic* missiles follow a ballistic, or unguided, trajectory like an artillery shell after the powered boost phase. These missiles may undergo later minor corrections in mid-course or during reentry from space. *Cruise*, or airbreathing, missiles fly like small aircraft and may take a preset but devious course to the target at low altitude. In principle, either of these missiles can be launched from underground launch-tubes, or *silos*, or from submarines, surface ships, or aircraft.

Over the years, the accuracy of all delivery missiles has greatly improved. This does much more than increases in explosive power to improve the effectiveness of weapons against specific targets. Whether manned or unmanned, delivery vehicles can be guided by *gyroscopes*, which make the vehicle aware of its movements after being launched from a known location. Still, errors can occur because of defects in the calculating machinery itself, uncertainty about the exact geographical relationship of the launch site and the target, and deflection by winds and gravitational pull. Such errors can be corrected, however, by information gained from stars or satellite navigational devices or from prestored ground information, which the satellite's guidance system senses by radar. A missile's measure of accuracy is its Circular Error Probable (CEP), which is the radius of the circle within which 50 percent of the shots are expected to fall. In today's most advanced systems, this error can now be reduced to about 165 feet (50 m).

Nuclear weapons are also classified according to their *range*. Usually weapons with a range of more than 3,000 miles (5,000 km) are classed as *intercontinental*, or Intercontinental Ballistic Missiles (ICBM). Weapons of between 600 and 3,000 miles (1,000-5,000 km) in range are usually classed as *intermediate* (IRBM), or *theater*, weapons because they would be used in a particular theater of war, such as Europe or East Asia. Weapons of intermediate range on submarines (Submarine Launched Ballistic Missiles, or SLBM) or on aircraft (Air Launched Cruise Missiles, or ALCM) are usually classed with the intercontinental weapons as *strategic*. Some SLBMs with a range of more than 3,000 miles (5,000 km) are now coming into service. Finally, weapons of up to 600 miles (1,000 km) are usually classed as *tactical*, or *short-range*, weapons. These can vary from the full 600-mile (1,000-km) missiles to the 6-to-9-mile (10-15-km) *battlefield* weapons such as artillery shells. There are also nuclear mines for use on land or at sea and, of declining importance, nuclear anti-aircraft missiles.

Page 13 (top to bottom):
The 18,700 – ton U.S.S. Ohio built to carry 24 Trident missiles.

Tomahawk SLCM/GLCM cruise missile – nuclear land attack version.

With a range of 6,000 miles (9,660 km), the Trident II is the U.S. Navy's largest SLBM.

Medium-range, intermediate-range, and intercontinental ballistic missiles are all capable of strategic roles and differ most significantly from each other in terms of range. However, the IRBM and ICBM are generally fitted with more advanced penetration aids (penaids) and multiple warheads.

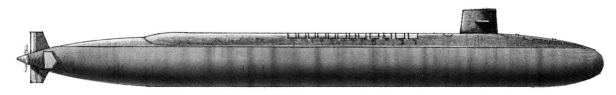

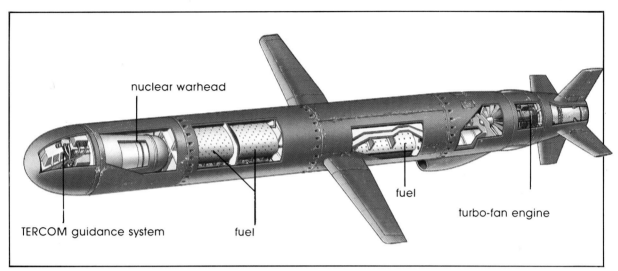

nuclear warhead

TERCOM guidance system

fuel

fuel

turbo-fan engine

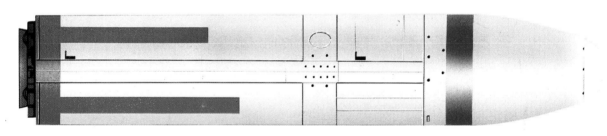

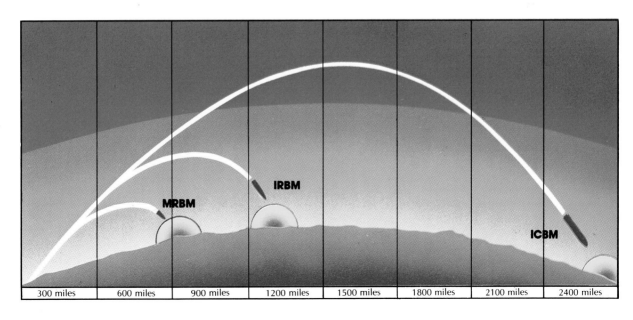

MRBM

IRBM

ICBM

| 300 miles | 600 miles | 900 miles | 1200 miles | 1500 miles | 1800 miles | 2100 miles | 2400 miles |

The Three-part Deterrent

The larger nuclear powers have maintained some weapons in each of the three launch categories: aircraft, land-based missiles, and sea-based missiles. This "triad" complicates the tactical problems of a would-be enemy and provides insurance against technical failure of any one of the weapon types.

Each of these delivery methods has special strengths and weaknesses. The land-based ICBM is easy to maintain and to control, but it is relatively vulnerable to attack because of its fixed and known location. The submarine-based missile is relatively invulnerable – antisubmarine warfare methods are not yet capable of reliably locating submarines – but it is less accurate because it is not easy for a submarine to know its exact location or to communicate without revealing its whereabouts. Aircraft are vulnerable on the ground and find it difficult to penetrate defenses. They are, however, capable of carrying large loads and, unlike ballistic missiles, can be recalled after launching.

The elements of this triad are not self-contained, and they can be used together to provide new capabilities. Aircraft, for instance, can carry missiles that make it unnecessary to penetrate all of the way to the target, which gives them a "stand-off" capability. Ballistic missile reentry vehicles with the ability to undertake limited maneuvers and carry more than one warhead have developed into the Multiple Independently Targetable Reentry Vehicle (MIRV), which is capable of attacking a number of separate targets. MIRVs can also assist in penetrating any forms of defense against ballistic missiles.

In the future we may see the deployment of Maneuverable Reentry Vehicles (MARV) which will be able to make major alterations of course in the very final moments before impact or detonation. Such maneuvers could be used to evade defenses and make interception more difficult. They could also permit last minute corrections of course using terrain mapping or other sensors. This could compensate for errors in navigation and provide almost perfect accuracy. It would probably be impossible to harden a missile silo, for instance, to such a degree as to remain operational after a direct nuclear hit.

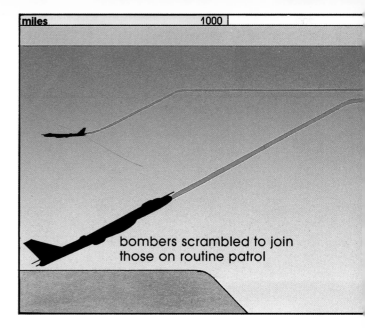

miles   1000

bombers scrambled to join those on routine patrol

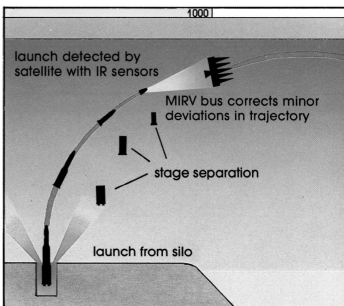

1000

launch detected by satellite with IR sensors

MIRV bus corrects minor deviations in trajectory

stage separation

launch from silo

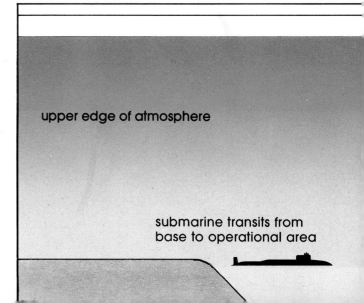

upper edge of atmosphere

submarine transits from base to operational area

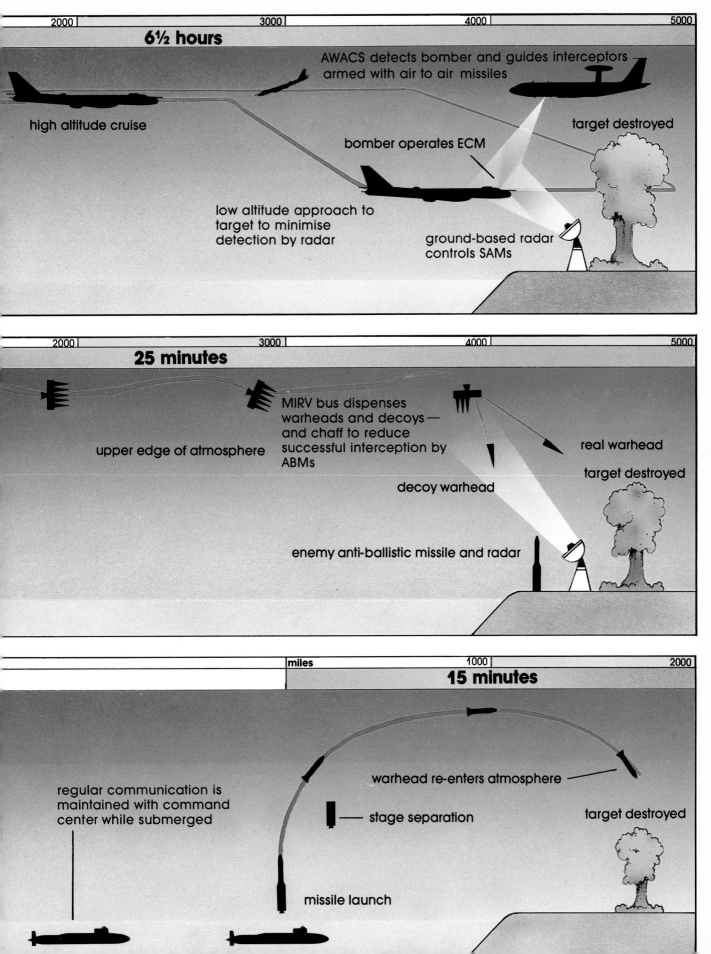

6½ hours

2000 | 3000 | 4000 | 5000

AWACS detects bomber and guides interceptors armed with air to air missiles

high altitude cruise

target destroyed

bomber operates ECM

low altitude approach to target to minimise detection by radar

ground-based radar controls SAMs

25 minutes

2000 | 3000 | 4000 | 5000

MIRV bus dispenses warheads and decoys — and chaff to reduce successful interception by ABMs

upper edge of atmosphere

real warhead

target destroyed

decoy warhead

enemy anti-ballistic missile and radar

15 minutes

miles | 1000 | 2000

regular communication is maintained with command center while submerged

warhead re-enters atmosphere

target destroyed

stage separation

missile launch

Land-based Missiles

The most common delivery system for nuclear weapons today is the ballistic missile, a rocket that follows a pre-set *trajectory*, or course, to its target. While earlier missiles had to be fueled just before launching – a process often taking hours and, therefore, a period of great vulnerability to attack – modern fuels permit almost instant readiness to fire. Today, rockets are powered either by liquid fuels that can be stored in the rocket or by solid fuels, and they can be launched in the few minutes it takes to set the course and open the doors of the missile tube, or silo.

A typical missile leaves its silo and climbs with energy from several stages of rocket fuel, discarding empty fuel casings for three or four minutes until reaching its cruising speed. After this *boost phase*, the warhead cruises through space for some 15 to 20 minutes. If it has *multiple warheads* that are destined for several targets – *i.e.*, one with Multiple Independently Targeted Reentry Vehicles, or MIRVs – a carrier, or *bus*, maneuvered by small rocket jets releases each Reentry Vehicle (RV) on its own ballistic course. Along with the warheads may go lightweight, false decoy warheads or *chaff* (radar-reflective strips) to confuse any defenses. Finally, the reentry period of two or three minutes occurs when, shielded against the heat generated by friction with the air, the RV reenters the atmosphere. During a flight of about 7,000 miles (11,000 km) and one-half hour, the RV will have reached an altitude of up to 1,000 miles (1,600 km).

For decades, ballistic missiles have also been used at shorter than strategic ranges, and modernized forms with much greater accuracy have emerged in recent years. These missiles are often less vulnerable because they are mobile – or at least movable – and are mounted on transporters and accompanied by firing and control facilities. The most famous example of this missile is the Soviet SS20 (opposite). Its deployment stimulated a complete rethinking of the nuclear balance in Europe and resulted in the deployment of the Pershing II (below).

Another approach to the problems of penetrating defenses and achieving prelaunch invulnerability has been the development of advanced cruise missiles. Based on the unmanned aircraft of the German *V-1* in World War II, today's cruise missiles have greatly improved motors, guidance systems, and warheads offering relatively cheap, accurate delivery systems that can be used for a variety of military missions with either nuclear or conventional warheads.

Below: Pershing II provides the U.S. Army in Europe with a capable theater weapon that can be moved around on its transporter and then be rapidly deployed and launched.

Right: The Soviet SS20 mobile ballistic missile with a three warhead MIRV represented technological upgrade of capability in the intermediate range so great as to open up wholly new, selective tactical options.

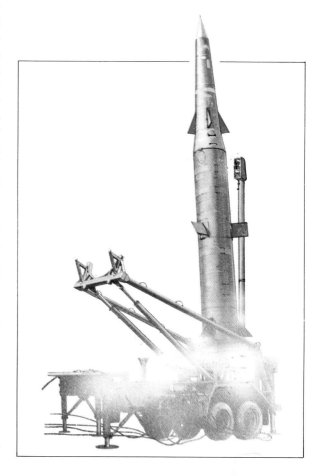

Above: Cruise missiles attracted most public attention, particularly in Europe, when U.S. Ground Launched Cruise Missiles became the major part of NATO's response to the Soviet Union's SS20. All of these weapons are destined to be destroyed under the Soviet - American Arms Control Treaty of 1987.

Air-to-Surface Missiles and Bombers

Manned bombers are the oldest type of vehicle used for modern strategic bombing missions. They possess the advantages of a high payload, good control (depending on the crew's capacity to respond to orders and to assess situations), and, if they survive a mission, reusability. Offsetting these advantages is the greatly improved performance of modern air defenses, which is due to up-to-date surveillance techniques and effective antiaircraft missiles and interceptors.

There are several approaches a bomber can take to penetrate a defense. One is a change in tactics. For instance, aircraft today usually attack at very low altitude in order to avoid detection and prolonged visibility to defenses. But this is expensive in fuel use and puts great strain on the crew and on the aircraft. An alternative is to equip the craft with ballistic or cruise *standoff missiles* to fly the final stages. Both aircraft and cruise missiles can also benefit from modern guidance which periodically checks the terrain below against an image that has been prestored by reconnaissance satellites. The vehicle can thus be guided to a final checkpoint and from there can set a final course for its target.

There is great excitement about a third approach to penetration: making the aircraft or cruise missile less visible to detection. Very modern and still highly secret *stealth techniques* – such as reshaping the vehicle to reduce radar echoes, suppressing heat sources that are vulnerable to infrared detection, using radar-absorbent materials and paint, and equipping the vehicle with active and passive electronic devices to suppress or distort radar images – have shown great promise. They have given new life to bombers and other aircraft once thought to be on the verge of obsolescence and have greatly improved the penetration capability of the small cruise missiles.

Below: The Soviet Union still uses turbo-prop Bears as strategic bombers but also has modern aircraft like the Mach 2.3 Blackjack and the Mach 2.0 Backfire, which is also used for naval tasks. These aircraft and cruise missiles are increasing the role of the Soviet Air Force in strategic delivery.
Page 19 (top): The terrain-comparison (Tercom) guidance of U.S. cruise missiles. At predetermined times during the flight, the Tercom is turned on to gain a digitally processed image of a presurveyed major landmark, and this is compared with a stored image so that the onboard computer can issue course corrections. The process is repeated several times to keep the deviation from the planned trajectory to a minimum and so give the missile excellent terminal accuracy.
Page 19 (bottom): Modernization and addition of standoff missiles have given the U.S. B52 a prolonged lease on life. It has recently been joined by the B1B.

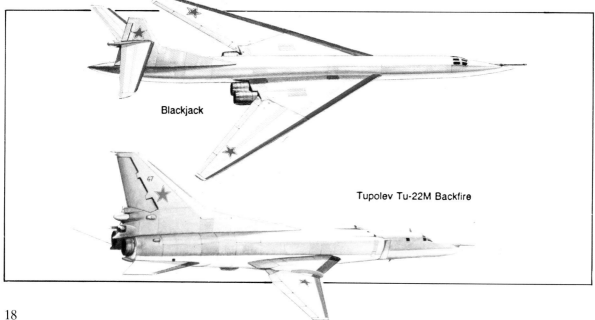

Blackjack

Tupolev Tu-22M Backfire

Rockwell International B-1B

Boeing B-52, Stratofortress

Sea-launched Missiles

The vulnerability of missiles to attack before launching led to building hardened silos for ICBMs. Another solution has been to put missiles in nuclear propelled submarines. These submarines are very difficult to detect, especially when they are able to cruise for weeks without surfacing. Today some 200 ballistic missile submarines (Submarines-Ballistic-Nuclear, or SSBNs) are in the U.S., Soviet, British, French and Chinese forces, which has stimulated great efforts in antisubmarine warfare (ASW).

Submarine-Launched Ballistic Missiles (SLBMs) used to be inaccurate because the submarine, forced to remain below the surface, found it difficult to identify its exact position, and therefore, could not set an accurate course for the missile. Modern navigation devices and the possibility of building corrective guidance systems into the reentry vehicles themselves have greatly improved performance in this respect, however. As a result, the SLBM is the supreme example of a retaliatory nuclear weapon that is capable of "riding out" an attack and remaining ready to retaliate. This makes the SLBM system very attractive to small nuclear powers such as Britain and France who have to rely on very few weapons.

While improved SLBMs are able to keep targets in range over wider areas of ocean, SSBNs have become quieter and harder to detect. Indeed, SSBNs may be able to stay close to friendly coasts where hostile antisubmarine forces find it difficult to operate, and they can also hide under the Arctic ice. Therefore, although today's Soviet SS-N 23 missiles have ranges up to 5,000 miles (8,000 km), the U.S. Trident can travel 4,000 miles (6,400 km), bringing more than 16 million square miles (42 million sq. km) of ocean within firing range of Soviet targets.

So far, the SLBM has seemed to be the indisputable last resort against the loss of retaliatory forces to enemy attack. The Soviet Union is now developing missiles that will be mobile on land, but whether they can offer the same degree of invulnerability as SLBMs is not yet known. An incentive to make the effort, however, is the high cost of the sophisticated SSBN system and the skilled crews that are required to undertake the arduous and nerve-wracking underwater cruises. One approach

to reducing costs has been to build larger submarines that can carry more missiles. The Soviet Typhoon SSBN, for instance, carries 20 missiles with multiple warheads. Because of treaty agreements, this trend will reduce the U.S. SSBN force – which for decades numbered 41 – to 20 large Ohio-class submarines. Of these, only 12 could be at sea at the same time.

With more eggs in fewer baskets, new vulnerabilities to success in ASW are inevitable. So if arms control agreements reduce the number of missiles permitted, there might be a return to smaller submarines.

Top left: The Soviet Delta III SSBN now carries the SSN-17 missile with 3 MIRV.
Below: The huge new 25,000 – ton Soviet Typhoon SSBN is the world's largest submarine. It carries 20 SSN 20 missiles with a range of over 4,800 miles (8,000 km).

3 The Control of Nuclear Forces

Early-warning Systems

The destructiveness of nuclear weapons, and the danger of escalation to higher levels of warfare if even one or two were used, makes governments possessing nuclear weapons anxious to guarantee their use only when absolutely necessary. Governments also want to be sure that their armed forces only use the weapons exactly as they were intended in order clearly to communicate any desire to keep the war limited. In addition to the need to keep military forces under political control, the military commanders themselves want to be particularly well-informed about the activities of this overwhelmingly powerful part of their forces. Consequently, great care has been taken to perfect the systems that control nuclear weapons, and systems for Command, Control, and Communication, or C^3 – to which is sometimes added Intelligence about friendly and hostile nuclear forces, or C^3I – are the fastest–growing elements of nuclear spending.

Closely connected to this system for controlling friendly forces are the systems used to determine the size and capabilities of potentially hostile forces and to provide warning of an impending attack.

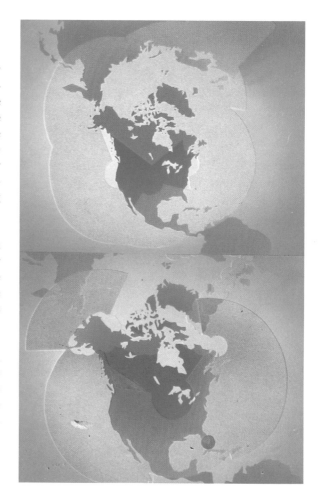

Top: An impression of the coverage provided by U.S. early warning radars. The ABM Treaty requires this coverage to be facing outwards from the national peripheries so as not to provide battle management capability for ABM defence. Three Ballistic Missile Early Warning Systems (BMEWS) in Alaska, Greenland, and the UK are left over from an earlier period, but a controversial modernization program to phased array is now being planned.

Bottom: U.S. radar coverage against air attack, a facility somewhat neglected while Soviet bomber forces were weak, but now more essential as the Soviet Union acquires new aircraft and cruise missiles. New Over the Horizon (OTH) radars provide cover up to 1800 miles (2,800 km).

Page 23 Far right: A modern U.S. radar station in the north with phased arrays replacing the more familiar mechanically rotated antennae. Warning is one of the most vital elements in determining the effectiveness of a defence as time eases the demands on the interceptor system.

Most of these activities are now performed by the many kinds of sensors carried by space satellites and by ground-based radars such as the three U.S. Ballistic Missile EarlyWarning Systems (BMEWS) that are located in Alaska, Greenland, and England.

The systems for preventing unintended use of nuclear weapons can be divided into three categories: safety devices to prevent accidental explosions or launching of weapons, laws and military discipline for making sure that people obey orders, and devices to prevent people from acting without authority.

While military discipline is nothing new, the special dangers of nuclear weapons have inspired ingenious physical controls. Thus, many weapons are *two-key*, requiring the cooperation of at least two operators for activating and launching. Weapons are also being fitted with electronic locks that require the insertion of a code number before operators can act. These Permissive Action Links (PAL) are often supplemented by devices that will make the weapon unusable if anyone tries to bypass the locks. Although many even more sophisticated physical controls are possible in principle – for instance, weapons could be designed to operate only on certain targets – the trade-off between safety, control, and usability has to be recognized. For instance, if a frontline artilleryman has to wait until his nuclear shells are brought to him by truck, there is no danger of his using the weapon beforehand. But such a system would also risk having the shells not reach the gun by the time the proper authorities wanted it used.

Surveillance Satellites

Nothing has done more to revolutionize military reconnaissance and surveillance than the new capability to put sensors in space. Satellites provide their owners with much information about the activities of other countries and also provide useful reassurance that nothing too dangerous is happening or that an attack is not imminent. The Strategic Arms Limitation (SALT) agreements between the Soviet Union and the United States were only possible because satellites provided a means of verifying compliance without imposing intrusive on-the-spot inspection. If nuclear war were tragically to occur, satellites could help to control it by providing reliable information about what was actually happening and therefore, could reduce the typical confusion that is often referred to as the "fog of war."

Below: This diagram gives a general impression of types of orbit employed by satellites for various purposes. Information can now be passed so quickly and in such quantities that any acquired by a satellite could, in principle, be virtually instantly available to its operators on the ground.

Right: The U.S. currently places high priority on strengthening communications between sensors, commanders and weapons. This illustration shows satellites for warning and communication, airborne links, warning radars and land mobile command posts. It also indicates the various radio links which provide duplication and the capacity to reorganize the system and reroute messages according to the resources available during failure or attack.

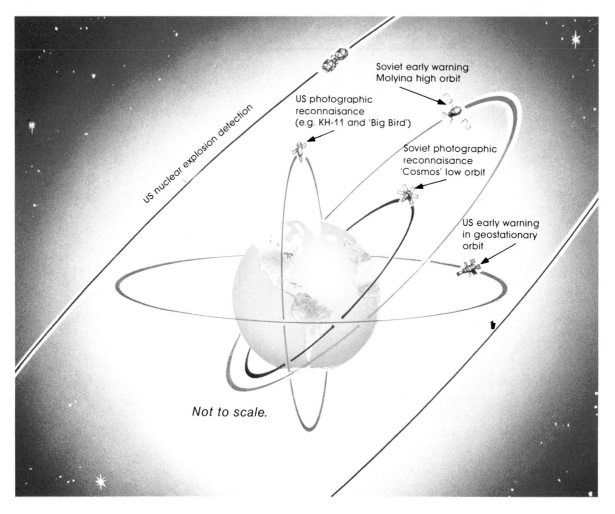

US nuclear explosion detection

US photographic reconnaisance (e.g. KH-11 and 'Big Bird')

Soviet early warning Molyina high orbit

Soviet photographic reconnaisance 'Cosmos' low orbit

US early warning in geostationary orbit

Not to scale.

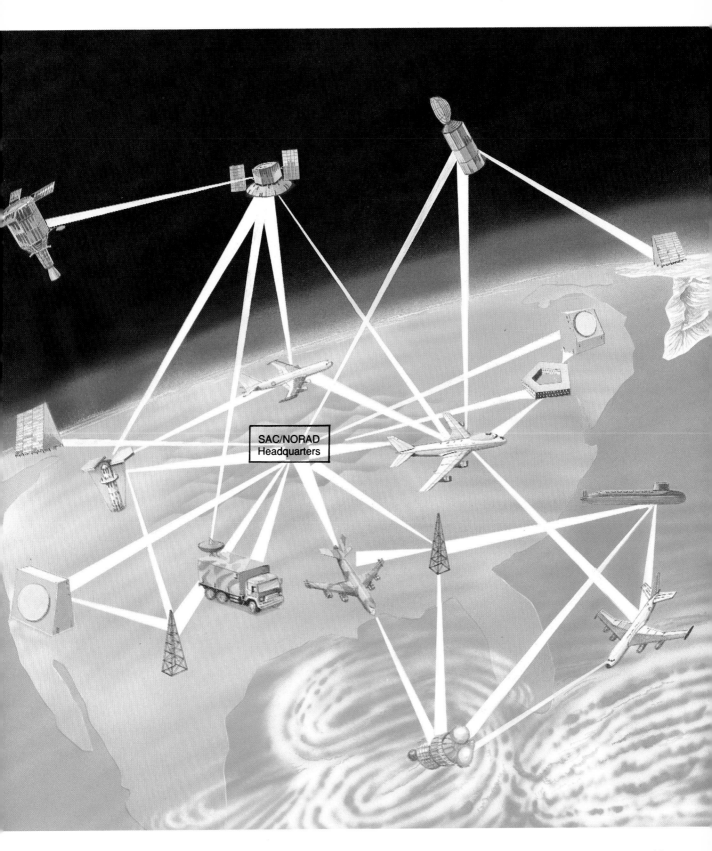

SAC/NORAD
Headquarters

Antimissile Weapons

Although strategic bombing – the long-range bombardment of enemy cities and industry – was an important feature of the Second World War, it did not prove to be as decisive as many had expected. Large numbers of high-explosive weapons were needed in order to achieve massive effects, and their delivery depended on using huge fleets of aircraft that were quite vulnerable to anti-aircraft defenses, especially to interceptor aircraft.

Now nuclear weapons have completely altered this situation in two ways. First, it takes only a very few of the larger nuclear weapons to create great destruction. Secondly, powerful nuclear warheads are now only a few feet in length so they can be delivered by ballistic missiles, which cannot be stopped by traditional air defenses. For many years, it was thought that no defense was possible against ballistic missiles, but now the situation has changed. This is an important development because the revolution created by nuclear weapons would be significantly reversed if effective defenses against missiles were to be developed.

As early as the late 1950s, developments in rocketry and in electronic guidance made it poss- ible for one rocket to intercept another and destroy it. But while it was possible to intercept single test rockets, catching all of a numerous incoming attack still seemed impossible. As it only took a few penetrations to cause a disaster, U.S. experts did not think building a defensive network was worth the great expense. (The Russians, however, built a defensive system around Moscow that still exists.)

A further reason to be doubtful about ballistic missile defenses then was the probable ease with which an attacker could make the defender's job more difficult. Although the most expensive, the simplest way would be to buy more offensive missiles to "saturate" the defense. Cheaper ways would be to equip reentry vehicles with devices such as chaff and decoys – lightweight imitations that acted like the real thing while outside the atmosphere – to confuse the defensive radar.

There are also broader arguments against ballistic missile defenses, and one is that such defenses could accelerate an arms race. Many people believe that if all parties in a nuclear balance of power know they have no defense, they will be cautious and content with fairly small attacking forces. But if an attacker faced with defenses, tries to get through by increasing the size of its attack, the result might be more rather than less destruction if the defenses failed. On the other hand, if one side were confident in its defense, it might be more tempted to use its own offensive forces. It was this kind of thinking that led the two Superpowers to sign the Anti-Ballistic Missile (ABM) Treaty of 1972. That treaty limited each side to one defended area like the one around Moscow, but the United States has yet to build the system permitted by the treaty.

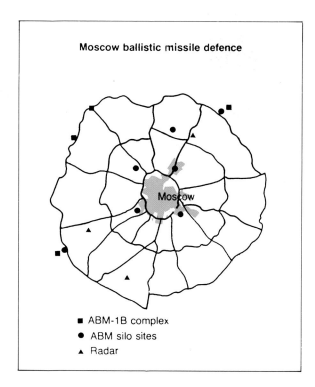

Moscow ballistic missile defence

Moscow

■ ABM-1B complex
● ABM silo sites
▲ Radar

Right: Some "Star Wars" approaches to anti-missile defenses include ground-based laser interception, space-based laser attack on missiles in early and late boost stages of both ICBM and SLBM, and anti-satellite hunter killers approaching target-acquiring components of the ABM force.

Left: The Soviet Union, unlike the United States deploys a missile defense around its national capital, Moscow.

Star Wars

Although the challenge of intercepting a reentry vehicle was technologically mastered in the 1960s, it still seemed impossible to offer a really worthwhile defense to a full-scale attack. By the 1980s, however, a variety of technological advances had made such a defense seem possible to both the Soviet Union and the United States. Because space operations played such an important role in these efforts, the U.S. program, officially called the Strategic Defense Initiative (SDI), became known as Star Wars.

Many different technologies contributed to this new optimism. Radars had become more efficient, and computers were much more capable of rapidly processing the information they received. Interceptor rockets could more quickly meet attacking warheads and, where earlier systems had to rely on nuclear explosions to destroy hostile reentry vehicles, more accurate interception made it possible to employ non-nuclear kill methods such as *conventional explosions* and shrapnel-like clusters of solid projectiles, or *kinetic kill*. The most Star-Wars-like idea was to use *laser beams* from the ground or from satellites to damage offensive vehicles. As rockets rose slowly and vulnerably from the ground with all their later-to-be-dispersed multiple warheads aboard, they might be destroyed by kinetic or laser devices in satellites over enemy launch-sites. These ideas offered the possibility of a *layered defense*, whereby the offensive force would be attacked during all three stages of its flight: the boost phase, the mid-course phase, and the reentry, or terminal, phase. Thus, the defense would have several chances to attack and could enjoy a good overall performance, even if each phase had been only partially successful.

There are still many difficulties with a layered defense, however, and many of the necessary devices are still in the experimental stage. It is particularly difficult to get the necessary energy for

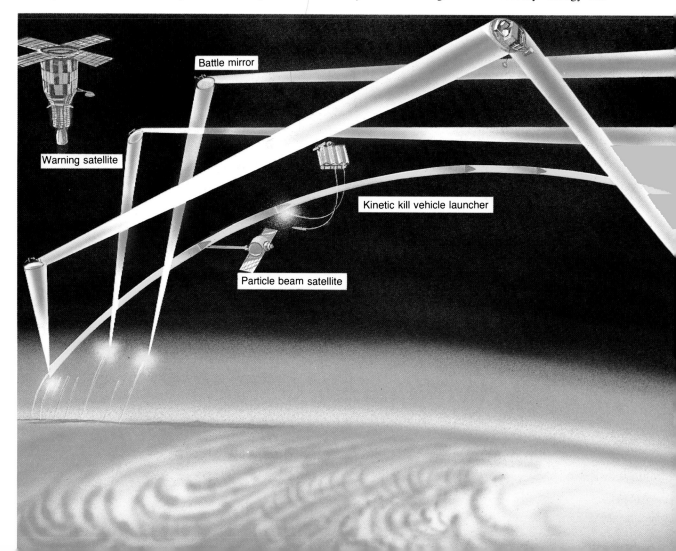

Battle mirror

Warning satellite

Kinetic kill vehicle launcher

Particle beam satellite

lasers into space because the atmosphere has the effect of shielding the ground. Moreover, the attacker can use countermeasures such as decoys and can "harden," or strengthen, its weapons against lasers. It can also increase the acceleration of its boosters to permit the separation of the war-heads while they are still within the atmosphere, which will give them some shielding from lasers. The enemy can, of course, also increase the attack by aircraft or cruise missiles, which means the defender must also have a good antiaircraft system.

Once an option becomes technologically poss-ible, its usefulness always depends on the cost. For instance, can an attacker afford to maintain the effectiveness of its attack? Most experts believe it will be a long time, if ever, before a "leak-proof umbrella of defense" can be built. But before then, defenses may become efficient enough to reduce an attacker's confidence in success and thus promote deterrence.

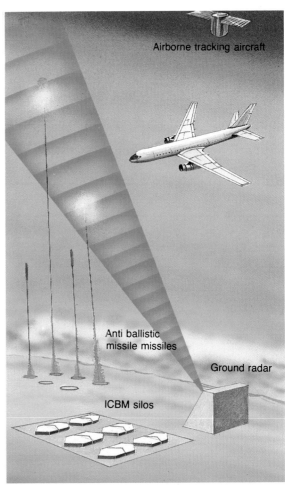

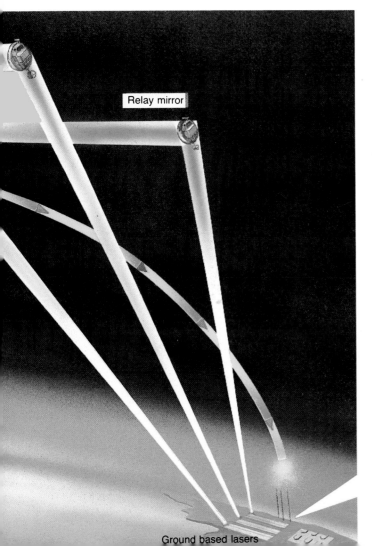

Above: A terminal defense defends ICBM silos. Reentry vehicles begin to decelerate in the atmos-phere and betray different characteristics from simple decoys at an altitude of about 60-70 miles (96-112 km). In this case satellite, airborne, and ground-based phased radars acquire, discriminate and track targets. Silo or mobile-based high acceler-ation interceptors rise to kill reentry vehicles in some two minutes. The kill mechanisms are probably non-nuclear.

Left: Components of a boost phase defense shows surveillance and tracking satellites, a ground-based laser using space-borne mirrors and a kinetic kill vehicle launcher. Boost to cruising speed takes some four to five minutes. In this case, a particle beam detector satellite makes observations to aid the defense. An effective boost defense would greatly reduce the advantages of MIRV and of decoys because neither would reach dispersal.

4 How Deterrence Might Fail

1 Early warning system detects nuclear attack.

2 NORAD confirms nuclear attack alert. Chiefs of staff and President informed.

3 Strategic air command bomber crews, ICBM's and SLBM's on full alert.

4 President consults with chiefs of staff. Final confirmation of nuclear attack.

Surprise Attack

The outbreak of nuclear war is usually imagined as a sudden all-out attack by one country on another in an effort to annihilate its armed forces, its industries, and, deliberately or not, its population. Why should a nation do this, especially with the danger of retaliation? The usual motive suggested is that the attacking country may fear it is about to be attacked. In such a situation, it might try to fore-

5 Nuclear-armed strategic air command bombers take off.

6 SLBM's are launched from submarines.

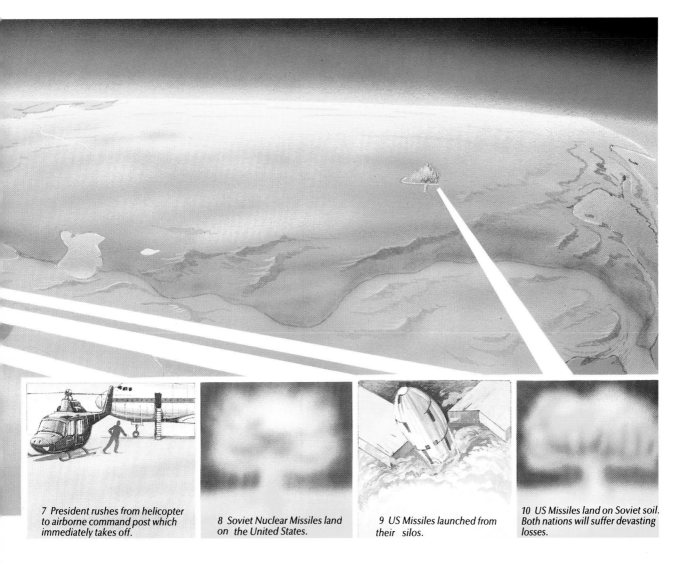

7 President rushes from helicopter to airborne command post which immediately takes off.

8 Soviet Nuclear Missiles land on the United States.

9 US Missiles launched from their silos.

10 US Missiles land on Soviet soil. Both nations will suffer devasting losses.

stall or preempt the attack, and, if it were optimistic, hope to eliminate retaliation. But, on the other hand, if the enemy were a major nuclear power that possessed a strong deterrent force, the best that could be hoped for would be an outcome for the attacker that would be better than if it had waited to be attacked first. The result, nevertheless, would be catastrophic, and the concern of those managing the nuclear forces would be their ability to retaliate and to maintain what is known as a secure, or safe, second strike.

If, on the contrary, the balance of forces reached a point at which one side believed the results of striking first were much better than waiting to retaliate, the situation might prove to be unstable. Even if the military balance had, theoretically, reached such a condition there still might not be war, for the risks and uncertainties would remain, and the consequences of making the wrong decision would be disastrous.

Limited Nuclear War

Although the common image of nuclear war is one of mutual destruction – probably in the form of a surprise attack followed by retaliation – that is not the only possibility. Some experts believe that nuclear wars could be controlled, or limited. Perhaps nuclear weapons might only be used on the battlefield to affect the course of an otherwise *conventional* operation. Or, perhaps, strategic, long-range weapons could be used only in limited sizes and numbers against military targets while trying to avoid populated areas, which would minimize casualties. In such a war, it would not be in the interest of either side to launch an all-out attack because that would give the other side no reason to withold *its* most destructive strike.

These possibilities raise many difficult questions.

As long as nuclear war *is* possible, some say that efforts should be made to develop the mechanisms of control and, above all, to realize that the use of a few nuclear weapons need not lead immediately to all-out destruction. Moreover, where the policy of nations – as in NATO – is that while they will try to defend themselves without nuclear weapons, they will use nuclear force rather than accept complete defeat and conquest, ways of limiting nuclear war are needed to prevent catastrophe and to make the deterrent threat believable.

Limited nuclear war, requires both very accurate weapons and extremely effective command and control systems. The flying command post shown below is one U.S. effort to provide for a few days of survival for the high command, even under the worst of conditions. By refueling and using extra crews, such aircraft could stay aloft until their

Boeing E-4B advanced airborne command post

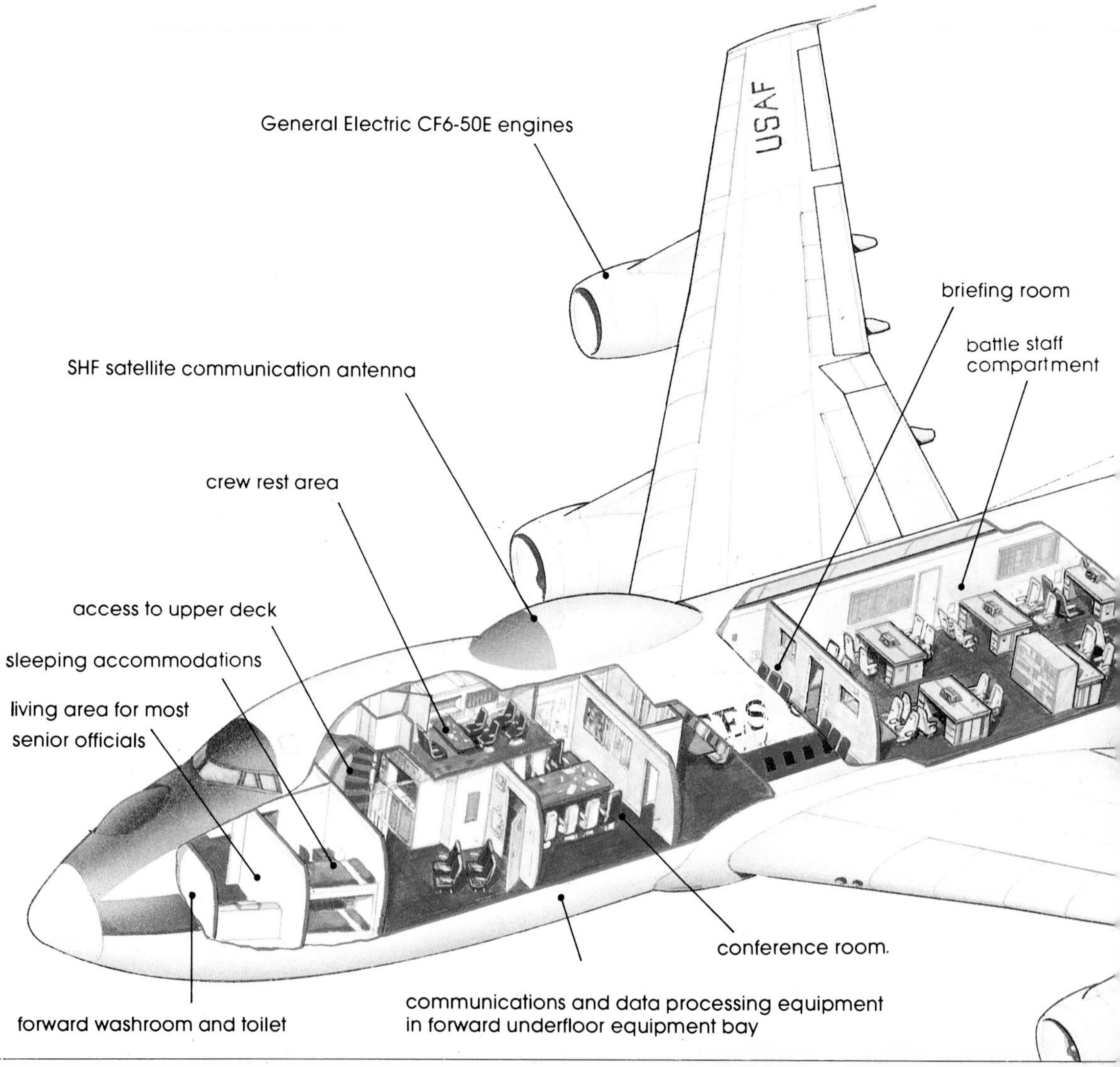

General Electric CF6-50E engines

USAF

briefing room

battle staff compartment

SHF satellite communication antenna

crew rest area

access to upper deck

sleeping accommodations

living area for most senior officials

forward washroom and toilet

conference room.

communications and data processing equipment in forward underfloor equipment bay lubricants wore out. But no one can be certain that such measures would be effective.

Indeed, many believe that limiting nuclear war is probably impossible. They fear any war would get out of hand because panic would lead to a loss of self-control among national leaders, and the resulting devastation would destroy the machinery for keeping command and control over the armed forces. While such chaos might lead to paralysis and, eventually, end the fighting, it could also lead to *escalation*, or a rise in the level of conflict, because subordinate commanders were out of control or weapons were used in haste for fear of enemy attack. This principle is flippantly known as "use it or lose it."

Those who are pessimistic about controlling nuclear war, but who accept the need for a national defense suggest that all conflicts should be handled with conventional weapons, which is sometimes called "raising the nuclear threshold." But as long as nuclear weapons exist or new ones can be made if the existing ones are destroyed, any war could turn nuclear. Moreover, a country prepared to defend itself against a conventional attack could still find itself under attack with nuclear weapons.

Given these possibilities, there are arguments between those who believe that raising the nuclear threshold would make the world safer and those who believe that knowing any sizable war could easily become nuclear would deter the outbreak of such wars. In theory, there is no way to settle this argument, but it does make clear that the prevention of nuclear war is closely related to the problem of trying to avoid *any* wars between nuclear powers.

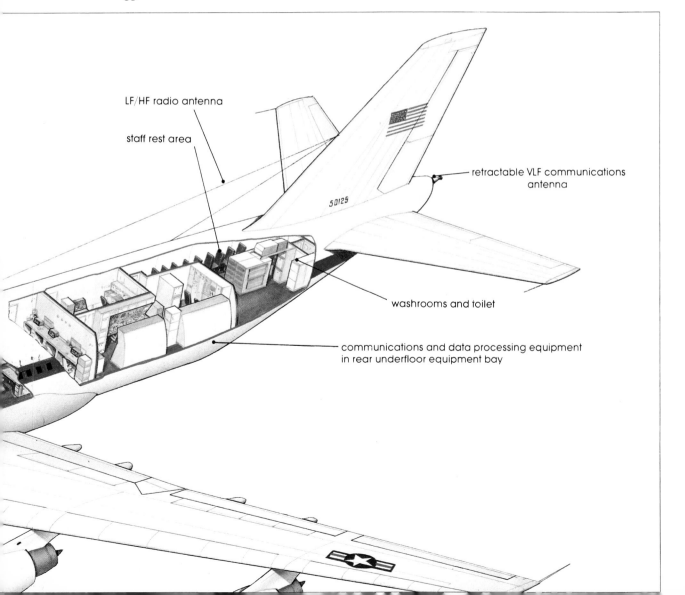

LF/HF radio antenna

staff rest area

50125

retractable VLF communications antenna

washrooms and toilet

communications and data processing equipment in rear underfloor equipment bay

War by New Nuclear Powers

Most of the discussion of how nuclear war might begin has centered on the two Superpowers. If nuclear weapons spread to other countries, the dangers of nuclear war would rise, partly because the systems and safeguards described here might not exist. Such *nuclear proliferation*, or growth, might also increase the danger of war for the following reasons:

1. The number of possible combinations of enemies equipped with nuclear weapons would increase.

2. Many of the nations thought to be close to acquiring nuclear weapons – like the two that may already have them, India and Israel – are involved in the relatively unstable quarrels of the Third World or have unstable internal political situations.

3. The existing five nuclear powers now have fairly well-developed nuclear forces and are rather closely locked into a deterrent balance with each other. Relationships between new nuclear powers with small and perhaps more vulnerable forces might be less stable.

One area in the world where the consequences of nuclear proliferation have long been feared is the Indian subcontinent. India and Pakistan have often been on bad terms for political and religious reasons and have already fought several wars, partly over their territorial dispute in Kashmir.

It is, therefore, easy to imagine tensions arising between India and Pakistan for reasons such as the Soviet resentment of Pakistani aid to the rebels in Afghanistan and renewed Indian intervention in the Kashmir dispute. The prospect of joint pressure from India and the Soviet Union would be very alarming to Pakistan and might force them to take military precautions against India. Then India, with Soviet support and much superior conventional forces, could decide to launch a preventive attack. Such a move might just force the Pakistani government to consider using a nuclear weapon to scare India into an armistice. Alternatively, India might fear such a Pakistani move and decide to strike first. If either of these events were to occur, the Superpowers might try to demand a ceasefire, as they would not want to be involved in a local nuclear war that could lead to very serious dangers worldwide.

34

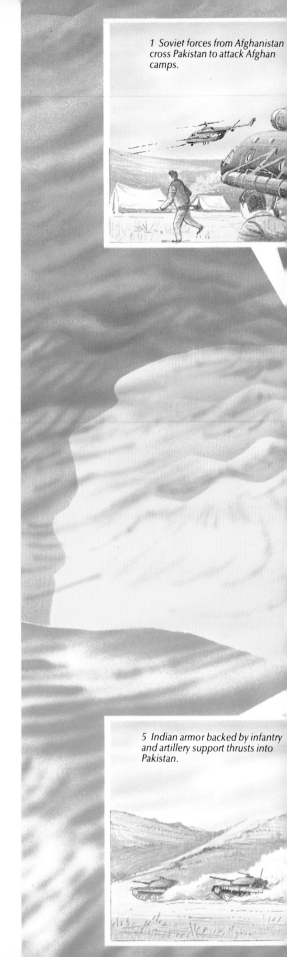

1 Soviet forces from Afghanistan cross Pakistan to attack Afghan camps.

5 Indian armor backed by infantry and artillery support thrusts into Pakistan.

2 Widespread rioting breaks out in Kashmir requiring Indian military intervention.

3 Indian forces pursue refugees/rebels over border into Pakistan.

4 Indian troops attempt to close Kashmir border with Pakistan. Clashes occur.

6 Conflict escalates and Indian numerical superiority takes its toll on Pakistan forces.

7 A crisis meeting of the Pakistan high command deliberates over the prospect of using nuclear weapons.

8 Pakistan might see a nuclear pre-emptive strike as the only course left open.

Nuclear Terrorism

So far in this nuclear age, nuclear weapons have been in the possession of only very few nations. While the danger of an increasing number of countries gaining possession of these powerful new weapons has long been recognized, much less attention has been given to the possibility that private groups might gain access to a nuclear weapon. In an age of widespread terrorism, it is not difficult to imagine the attraction that such a terrifying instrument might have for those seeking power for coercion or blackmail. In theory, terrorists might either seize an existing weapon or set up a secret organization to make one. Although there is no known example of any unofficial group having a nuclear weapon, many threats to acquire weapons have been made – mostly, no doubt, by cranks or hoaxers. But we do not know whether any of these threats have been taken seriously or have caused alarm in government circles because such events are kept secret.

On the whole, obtaining nuclear weapons by unauthorized individuals or groups seems unlikely because nuclear materials are difficult to acquire and to handle. Military weapons and nuclear power stations and manufacturing facilities are closely guarded, often by special police forces or by technological devices, and nuclear material is usually transported in special vehicles in heavily-guarded convoys. Also, nuclear weapons often contain mechanisms that not only prevent accidental explosions but also *spoil*, or disable, the weapon if an unauthorized person tampers with it.

Radioactive material is so dangerous, however, that it might not be necessary for terrorists to obtain a weapon. Instead, they could create immense fear and panic if they were only suspected of possessing a nuclear bomb and threatened to release radioactive material. As the amount of radioactive waste in the world increases, this might offer one of the easier targets for terrorists.

1 Terrorists seize train transporting nuclear waste.

5 Aftermath of Nuclear War

Immediate and Long-Term Effects

The detonation of nuclear weapons has a number of very powerful effects. Chief among them are the immediate release of X-ray energy followed by thermal radiation, atmospheric blast and the subsequent movement of longer-term radiation, which is carried in dust from the bomb and residue from any crater. These longer term aftereffects depend on the design of the weapon and how it was used – whether on the earth's surface or below the ground or in or above the atmosphere. The weather is also a factor. Wind can cause long-distance travel of particles, and fog can shield against thermal radiation.

The explosive nuclear components of a typical weapon instantly rise to temperatures of several million degrees, which is comparable to the temperature at the sun's center. By comparison, a chemical explosion might generate some 2,500 degrees Fahrenheit (5,000 degrees Celsius). Enormous pressures are generated when the bomb's components become gaseous. Within one millionth of a second, energy is released as the X-rays are absorbed by surrounding matter, and the well-known luminous "fireball" will appear if the explosion occurs in the atmosphere. (In space, however, the X-rays would not immediately be transformed into heat and blast but would travel long distances as X-rays.) The fireball from a one-megaton explosion in the atmosphere would rise several miles per minute, while the gases would begin to condense back into particles. Particles from the bomb would be supplemented by solid matter if the fireball had touched the ground and by water vapor if it had touched water. The clouds of radioactive particles that form, called *fallout*, could cause long-term damage over large areas. One percent of a one-megaton weapon's energy could create some 4,000 tons of fallout.

An explosion in the atmosphere also causes a shock wave of compressed air that travels at about one-half mile (1 km) in two seconds. This causes *over-pressure*, which is highest – about 16 pounds (7 kg) per square inch (6.5 cm^2) – at about 1.3 miles (2 km) from where the bomb was detonated, or *ground zero*. Here the first wave meets a reactive reflection. Thermal radiation also occurs, and animals up to some 12 miles (19 km) from ground zero can be burned.

Buildings will suffer damage chiefly from explosion and fire. The five-pounds-per-square-inch (2.3 kg/6.5 cm^2) over-pressure at four miles (6.4 km) results in a force of about 180 tons on the side of the average house. Buildings are also destroyed by fires caused by the thermal radiation. Although people are usually injured by the collapse of buildings rather than by the over-pressure, the various forms of radiation can also kill people, either quickly or slowly.

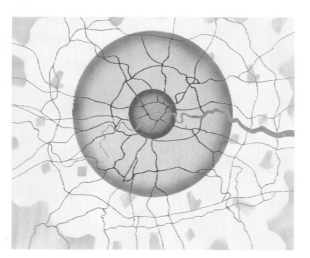

Left: The areas affected by a 1 MT airburst over London, centered on Westminster. The inner circle, of radius 5 miles, represents the regions suffering maximum structural damage and the outer circle shows the maximum extent of thermal radiation, which will cover a radius of 15 miles.

Right: Diagram shows the destructive effect of a 1 MT airburst. The significant prompt effects are thermal radiation and blast. The radii from ground zero are only approximations. Actual effects would vary considerably according to topography and meteorological conditions.

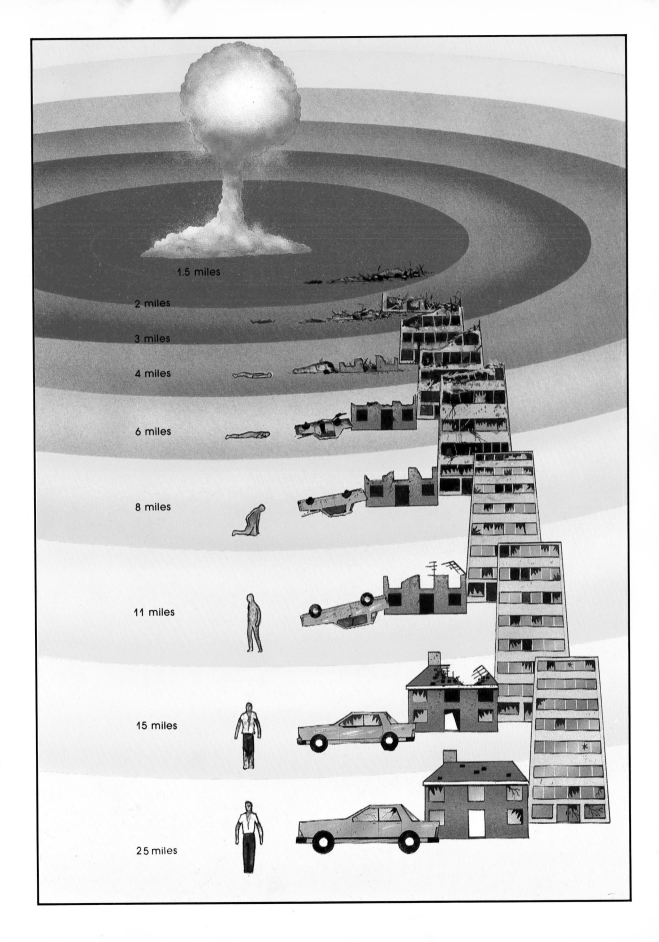

1.5 miles

2 miles

3 miles

4 miles

6 miles

8 miles

11 miles

15 miles

25 miles

Medical Effects and Civil Defense

The large-scale destruction caused by the radiation emitted by nuclear explosions – and to a lesser extent by nuclear material without an explosion – explains why nuclear weapons are regarded with such horror. There are four main types of nuclear radiation. *Alpha* and *beta particles* have little penetrating power and are unlikely to do harm unless they are swallowed or inhaled. *Gamma and X-rays*, however, can penetrate human skin and easily invade the body.

In daily life, everyone is exposed to radiation in various forms. Although higher-than-average doses in some areas and occupations can do great harm, humans usually survive this kind of radiation. All radiation, however, affects the body's electrical charges, which can make cells much more active and can accelerate their multiplication. For this reason, parts of the body already normally engaged in rapid self-replacement – such as blood, bone marrow, and the digestive system – are especially vulnerable to damage from the immensely high, atypical doses of radiation produced by a nuclear explosion. This damage may cause immediate vomiting or nausea – and early death – as well as the onset of various kinds of cancer or susceptibility to other longer term diseases. While some of these effects can be reduced by medical attention, medical facilities are likely to be disrupted and overburdened – or completely destroyed – during any sizable nuclear war.

Another danger feared by many is that a large-scale nuclear war could release so much smoke that the sun would be obscured. The resulting *nuclear winter* would make agriculture impossible for a season or more and bring about a famine.

How vulnerable people and their homes are to nuclear war depends on many circumstances, including the location of population and cities, the scale of the attack, and the degree of preparation. In the wars of this century since strategic bombing began, *civil defense* – efforts to make the target better able to survive the attack rather than to shoot down bombers – has been successful in reducing damage. Civil defense can include building shelters for people and efforts to improve medical facilities and other recovery preparations. While many people decided that civil defense was hopeless against nuclear attack, some countries such as the Soviet Union, Sweden, and Switzerland have continued to maintain civil defense programs.

In very recent years, there has been a revival of interest in civil defense for two reasons. First, given the horror of nuclear war, it is possible that a conventional war might be waged instead, and civil defense could play its traditional role. Secondly, there are those who believe the desire to avoid an all-out nuclear war might keep even a nuclear conflict limited, and, again, civil defense might be effective. Some governments, therefore, have tried to reawaken interest in building shelters and preparing for evacuation.

Many people, however, still remain doubtful about the success of civil defense efforts. There are also differences of opinion about the wisdom of such preparations, as many believe that making such preparations could help to bring on a war by making governments too confident about survival or by frightening other governments into believing that these are preparations for war. Today, the promise of better active defense – shooting missiles and bombers down before they can do damage – suggests that civil defense might have new value in the final line of protection against the surviving portion of the attack. Meanwhile, the basic argument continues. Is the world safer when people can defend themselves or when they fear that war would be the final disaster?

Right: The rate at which cells naturally multiply in the body is a major determinant of vulnerability to radiation damage. The diagram locates and rates the systems of the body in order of highest activity and, hence, of increased sensitivity.

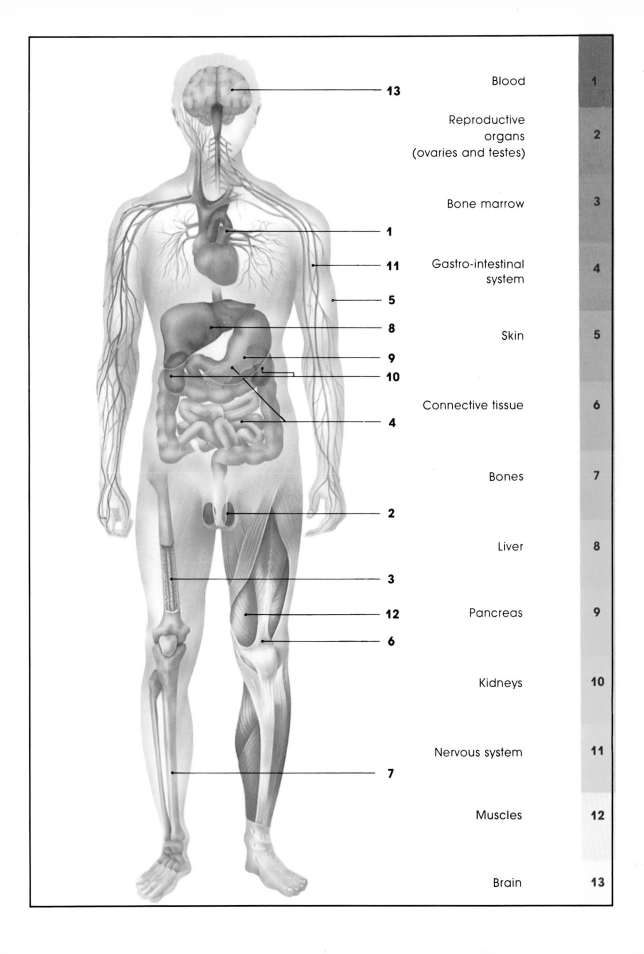

Blood	1
Reproductive organs (ovaries and testes)	2
Bone marrow	3
Gastro-intestinal system	4
Skin	5
Connective tissue	6
Bones	7
Liver	8
Pancreas	9
Kidneys	10
Nervous system	11
Muscles	12
Brain	13

6
The Way Ahead

Abolition and Disarmament

The dangers of nuclear weapons have brought about numerous peace movements, with members demanding various forms of disarmament. While these movements have had limited success in halting nuclear production, they have created powerful political pressures on governments. No government today dares be without a disarmament policy, and a nation's military activities are often subject to public debate and criticism.

In theory, there are only two ways to deal with the problem of nuclear weapons: abolish them or learn to live with them. President John F. Kennedy, who conducted U.S. policy during what was perhaps the world's most serious nuclear crisis, the so-called Cuban missile crisis, likened nuclear disarmament to the problem of "getting the nuclear genie back in the bottle." But if the genie could be put back inside, he would still be alive, and there would need to be some reassurance that he would not be let out again.

The abolition of nuclear weapons requires that countries be sure all weapons have been destroyed and no more will be made. Otherwise, what is often called the *armament race*, could become a *rearmament race*. This problem is made serious because those nations having even a few nuclear weapons would have tremendous political power over other nations. Thus, a system for abolishing nuclear weapons and keeping them abolished would require methods of reassuring nations that were hostile to each other and, perhaps, already at war with each other with conventional weapons.

Below: In December 1987 President Ronald Reagan and General Secretary Mikhail Gorbachev signed the historic INF disarmament treaty, which requires the destruction of some nuclear weapons.

So far, no agreement on the abolition of nuclear weapons has been reached. The United States once proposed that nuclear material should be used only for such peaceful activities as generating electric power, and should be internationally owned and subject to inspection and control. Their proposal, however, was rejected by the Soviet Union because the United States was not willing to surrender its nuclear weapons until the new system was in place. The Soviet Union regarded this as an attempt to bring a halt to its nuclear programs while the United States continued to keep a nuclear force while the control system – which might never come into existence – was being discussed.

Although world leaders continue to state that abolishing all nuclear weapons is their prime goal, no plans for actual abolition have gone very far in negotiations since the failure of these proposals. Meanwhile, there have been many efforts to reduce the number of nuclear weapons, and some progress has been made with the Strategic Arms Limitation agreements and the ABM Treaty between the Soviet Union and the United States. There are also treaties banning nuclear weapons in space, in Antarctica, and in one or two areas such as Latin America. These regional treaties do not, however, enjoy universal support.

In Soviet-U.S. negotiations on reducing strategic arms – which the U.S. now calls START (Strategic Arms Reduction Talks) – both sides have proposed reductions up to 50 percent, but until recently they had made little progress in putting their ideas into practice. The 1987 Soviet-U.S. agreement on intermediate-range nuclear weapons was however the first to bring about the abolition of a substantial number of already existing weapons. The hundreds of ballistic and cruise missiles involved, however, constitute less than 5 percent of the total nuclear weapons of the two countries.

Some people believe that the pace of technological change is outstripping arms control, and they would like to slow it down. One form of technical development is the testing of nuclear weapons, but testing in the atmosphere produces serious health hazards from radiation. Therefore, the Test Ban Treaty (TBT) forbidding the practice was signed in 1963, and almost every nation has accepted this treaty.

In an effort to slow the development of nuclear weapons and to prevent new nations from obtaining them, there is also much support for a Complete Test Ban Treaty (CTBT) that would outlaw underground testing. The two major obstacles to such a treaty have been the difficulty of verifiable checking and the belief of some scientists that testing is necessary to be sure that existing weapons are in working order.

The other main effort to prevent the spread of nuclear weapons has been the Non-Proliferation Treaty (NPT) of 1968. By this treaty, nonnuclear nations agree not to obtain nuclear weapons, and countries with nuclear weapons agree not to help them. The nuclear nations also promise to try to reduce their own forces and to assist the nonnuclear countries with the development of peaceful uses of nuclear energy.

When nuclear technology was new, it was widely believed that its proliferation, or spread, could be stopped by keeping the "secret of the bomb" from others. But now it is recognized that the basic ideas about how to make nuclear weapons are known to any competent physicist. Also, the spread of nuclear technology for peaceful purposes, including generating electricity and medical diagnosis and treatment, has trained many experts around the world. Any reasonably modern nation, therefore, could master making a bomb by using very high-quality engineering and some fissile material or uranium ore.

Nevertheless, most experts now believe the real barriers to nuclear proliferation are political, and that the solution lies in making it difficult for countries to acquire nuclear weapons. This requires creating a situation in which any nation that weighs the political and military benefits of having nuclear weapons against their cost in money, ill will from other countries, and the dangers of possessing nuclear weapons will decide not to go ahead. One factor, of course, is the extent to which nations believe they need nuclear weapons for self-defense. Guarantees of help from other governments or even a supply of conventional weapons might reduce the need for nuclear weapons. Thus, some activities that do not look peaceful at first – such as alliances or arms sales – may actually contribute to nonproliferation. This will only happen, however, if such actions do not make some other country that could obtain nuclear weapons feel insecure.

Arms Control

The lack of progress in disarmament – the abolition or reduction of the number of nuclear weapons – has led to support for *arms control*. Although arms control can include disarmament, its aim is to reduce the danger of arms used in war and to minimize the damage if war does recur. Some supporters of arms control argue that not only is total nuclear disarmament unlikely but that some reductions in weapons could be dangerous – for instance, if forces were reduced to the point at which nations would be vulnerable to surprise attack. In other words, successful deterrence serves the goals of arms control, and one of the purposes of arms control, failing complete disarmament, is to reinforce the stability of the deterrent balance.

The ABM Treaty, therefore, aims to stabilize deterrence by stopping one side from trying to escape retaliation. It actually clears the way for nuclear weapons to reach their targets in the hope that vulnerable countries would be careful not to start a nuclear war. Similarly arms control agreements that limit offensive missiles, as modestly achieved in the SALT agreements, have two purposes. The first is to reinforce deterrence by making it difficult to build a *first strike force* that could destroy an enemy's retaliatory force. Secondly, by limiting the number of weapons these agreements might reduce the likely damage that would occur if war came. But so far, the forces still permitted to exist could do catastrophic damage.

Arms control agreements and talks may also make the world safer by leading nuclear powers to believe their potential enemies want to avoid nuclear war. The Soviet Union and the United States hold regular meetings to discuss any behavior regarding nuclear weapons that either thinks could be dangerous.

The goals of arms control can also be pursued by one nation alone, or *unilaterally*, if it avoids building forces that are unsafe, hard to control, or likely to produce unnecessary anxiety on the part of other nations. An invulnerable retaliatory force capable of surviving counterforce attack but not designed to launch a counterforce attack itself could, therefore, be regarded as a contribution to arms control because it gives neither its owners nor its enemies reason to attack.

Nations may even take unilateral measures toward actual disarmament. The United States, for instance, has reduced the number of its nuclear weapons in recent years by more than 2,000. Whether or not such steps make the world safer remains open to argument.

Moreover, the problems of disarmament and arms control change as technology advances. With the appearance of MIRVs, it was no longer sufficient just to count missiles because what was inside a missile's reentry package could not be determined from a satellite. (It is, however, possible to determine if a missile is *tested* with the MIRVs, and some agreements provide that where one missile in a class is fitted with MIRVs, all missiles of that kind will be counted as being MIRVed.) In a similar situation, since the Russians developed the *cold launch*, which ejects the missile before the rockets ignite, the firing of a missile no longer destroys its silo. As the silo can be reloaded and reused, counting silos from satellites is no longer an accurate measure of the number of missiles. The problem of verification, therefore, is a major one in arms control, and the so-called *national means of verification* such as satellite photography and radar may need to be backed up by *on-site inspection*. The 1987 INF Treaty involved an unprecedented agreement to all such inspections.

Conclusion

Everyone has his or her own idea about how best to tackle the intensely serious problem of nuclear weapons. Some will work for their abolition, which is the declared ultimate goal of most world leaders. The difficulties of achieving this are very great, however, and careless or overeager efforts to achieve this goal might actually be harmful. While nuclear weapons are a great danger, they exist because the nations that own them think they provide some protection against serious threats to their security, some of which are also nuclear.

Most statesmen, therefore, believe that the day for abolishing nuclear weapons is far off and, meanwhile, nations must find safe ways to live with them. In effect, this is an arms control outlook that can be pursued both by trying to have cautious strategies and controllable weapons, safe from accidents, and by agreements about arms control. Under such an arrangement, governments would undertake to reduce the number of weapons and abolish dangerous ones and keep each other informed and reassured about situations that might otherwise cause countries to take hostile action.

Although nuclear weapons may not be eliminated in the near future, and the leading military blocks would find it difficult to reshape their military strategies without them, there does seem to be some change in thought regarding nuclear weapons. Governments seem to realize that they can make do with fewer weapons, that they could never use more than a few without suicidal consequences, and that they must work hard on their own policies and in agreements with others to make sure that, if the world remains nuclear, it does so in an increasingly limited and controlled way. While no single action will guarantee success, everyone seems to realize that failure would be catastrophic for everyone – everywhere – on this earth.

Nuclear Chronology

1945	April: First fission explosion test at Alamogordo, New Mexico August: Atomic bombing of Hiroshima and Nagasaki, Japan
1945	First Soviet atomic test
1952	First British atomic test
1953	First U.S. H bomb test
1953	First Soviet H bomb test
1953	United States adopts Massive Retaliation doctrine
1954	NATO incorporates nuclear weapons in war plans
1957	Soviet Union launches Sputnik space satellite British thermonuclear test
1960	French atomic test
1960	United Stated deploys Polaris, Minuteman missiles
1961	U.S. replaces Policy of Massive Retaliation with Flexible Response
1962	Cuban missile crisis
1963	Nuclear Test Ban Treaty
1964	Chinese nuclear test
1966	France leaves NATO military structure
1967	NATO adopts policy of Flexible Response Chinese thermonuclear test Soviet Union and United States deploy ABM systems
1968	French thermonuclear test
1970	U.S. deploys Minuteman III, Poseidon, MIRVs; Soviet Union deploys SS9, Yankee, Delta SSBN
1972	SALT I and ABM Treaties
1974	India explodes nuclear device
1974	United States adopts doctrines of limited nuclear war
1976	Soviet Union deploys SS17, SS18, SS19, MIRVs, SS20
1979	United States deploys Trident, cruise missiles; NATO modernizes INF
1983	United States begins Strategic Defense Initiative (Star Wars) research
1984	United States deploys B1, MX; Soviet Union deploys SS24/25 mobile ICBM
1987	U.S./Soviet Union agree to dismantle intermediate and shorter range missiles

Glossary

ACTIVE DEFENSE
Defense by interception of the attacking weapons or vehicles; see passive defense

ALPHA PARTICLE
Stable group of two protons and two neutrons emitted during radioactive decay

ARMAMENT RACE
Competition between two or more competitors to achieve military superiority, particularly by amassing a large number of weapons

ARMS CONTROL
Efforts whether unilateral or by negotiation between two nations to minimize the likelihood of war or of its destructive consequences if it occurs, sometimes but not necessarily by reductions or limitations of arms.

ATOM
The smallest unit of a chemical element composed of more elementary particles

ATOMIC BOMB
A bomb in which the explosive energy is derived from the splitting of atoms of uranium or plutonium

BALLISTIC MISSILE
Missile that, after a brief phase of powered flight, follows an unpowered trajectory like an artillery shell

BALLISTIC MISSILE SUBMARINE
A submarine armed with ballistic missiles normally capable of being fired from a submerged position

BATTLEFIELD WEAPON
Weapon intended for use in close proximity to contending armies as distinct from those aimed at the rear areas or homelands of combatants

BETA PARTICLE
A fast particle emitted during the radioactive decay of a nucleus

BIPOLAR
In politics or strategy, a relationship, usually antagonistic, between or dominated by two major powers

BOOST PHASE
The period during which a ballistic missile is accelerated by its motors

CHAFF
Short lengths of reflective material dispersed in clouds to confuse radar

CHAIN REACTION
The process by which nuclear decay produces particles which cause further nuclear reactions

CHEMICAL REACTION
The process by which chemical compounds transform one another into different compounds

CIVIL DEFENSE
Measures taken to protect the civilian population, homes, and industry of a nation from attack

COLD LAUNCH
A technique by which a missile is ejected from its silo by compressed air, after which the rocket motor is ignited. The technique slightly improves the throw-weight of the missile and allows the silo to be reused.

CONVENTIONAL EXPLOSION
Explosion dependent on a chemical reaction

CONVENTIONAL WAR
War not employing nuclear weapons. The term sometimes also excludes chemical warfare.

COUNTERATTACK
An attack launched by a defender in response to a previous assault

COUNTERMEASURE
A measure intended to neutralize a defensive operation or device

COUNTER-FORCE STRIKE
Attack on the offensive strategic forces of an enemy

CRITICAL MASS
Minimum quantity of radioactive material capable of sustaining a chain reaction by means of nuclear fission

CRUISE MISSILE
A missile that flies supported by wing or body lift

DECOY
In strategic weapons, a lightweight and cheap imitation of a real warhead intended to confuse the defense

DISARMAMENT
The process of reducing the number of or eliminating weapons

DETERRENCE
A policy of discouraging an attack by threatening an overwhelming response

DUAL-KEY SYSTEM
Physical system to assure two or more nations' control over final decision to use nuclear weapons during time of war, which allows for consultation among allies on the decision to resort to a nuclear attack

ESCALATION
The process by which the level of violence in combat increases whether unintentionally or as a deliberate attempt to bring pressure on the enemy

FALLOUT
Radioactive material falling from the atmosphere, usually as a result of a nuclear explosion

FIREBALL
The luminous sphere of hot gases at the center of a nuclear explosion

FIRST STRIKE
The initial blow in nuclear conflict; see second strike

FISSILE MATERIAL
Either uranium or plutonium that is in a form that can be utilized in nuclear reactors or nuclear weapons. Fissile material for nuclear weapons is referred to as *weapons grade*

FISSION
The splitting of an atomic nucleus

FREE-FALLING BOMB
Unpowered and unguided bomb dropped from an aircraft by gravity

FUSE
Device for detonating a weapon

FUSION
The creation of an atomic nucleus by the union of two lighter nuclei

GAMMA RAY
Electromagnetic radiation emitted during radioactive decay

GROUND ZERO
The point on the earth over which a nuclear weapon is detonated

HOT LAUNCH
The ignition of a missile's motors within the silo

HYDROGEN BOMB
Weapon deriving its energy from the fusion of hydrogen nuclei

INERTIAL GUIDANCE
An onboard guidance system; based on precise measurement of the accelerations experienced by a vehicle

INTERCONTINENTAL-RANGE MISSILE
Land-based missile typically capable of traveling over 3,000 miles (5,000 km)

INTERMEDIATE-RANGE MISSILE
Missile typically with a range between 600–3,000 miles (1,000–5,000 km)

KINETIC KILL
Capability for destroying a target by the impact of solid material

LASER BEAM
(Light Amplification by Stimulated Emission of Radiation) Device producing an intense beam of coherent light

LAYERED DEFENSE
Defense comprising several distinct layers of obstacles or countermeasures, each complementing the effect of the others

LOW LEVEL PENETRATION
Flight profile of aircraft designed to minimize detection by ground-based radars

MID-COURSE PHASE
The period of a ballistic missile's flight between the boost phase and the reentry phase

MULTIPLE WARHEAD
Warhead containing more than one reentry vehicle, thereby capable of attacking a number of targets simultaneously

NATIONAL MEANS OF VERIFICATION
Term used in arms control treaties to identify devices such as satellites and radar that can acquire military information without the

direct cooperation of the nation being inspected; see on-site inspection

NUCLEAR ENERGY
Energy released during the reactions of atomic nuclei

NUCLEAR POWER
Electrical power generated by the use of nuclear reactions, typically by using the heat created to produce steam

NUCLEAR PROLIFERATION
The spread of nuclear weapons to additional countries

NUCLEAR REACTION
The process in which atomic nuclei react with each other to produce changes in structure and the release of energy

NUCLEAR WAR
War employing nuclear weapons

ON-SITE INSPECTION
Examination of military establishments by direct inspection; see national means of verification

OVERPRESSURE
The excess pressure over normal atmospheric pressure which results from the rush of air displaced from the site of an atomic explosion. It is measured in pounds per square inch (psi)

PASSIVE DEFENSE
Measures taken to minimize the effect of an attack on a target; e.g., by hardening or concealment; see active defense

PAYLOAD
Total mass of a missile's warheads, together with their associated arming, fusing, and safety systems, penetration aids, and any other device that is carried to the target

PRE-EMPTIVE ATTACK
An assault started on the basis of evidence that an enemy attack is about to take place

REENTRY PHASE
The phase during which a warhead reenters the atmosphere; see terminal phase

RETALIATION
Military operations conducted in response to an attack, sometimes, but not necessarily, of the same kind

SECOND STRIKE
Strike launched by a nuclear force that has already suffered an attack

SHORT-RANGE BALLISTIC MISSILE
Missile typically with a range of between 300–600 miles (500–1,000 km)

SILO
Underground chamber, usually extremely strong, housing a ballistic missile

STAND-OFF MISSILE
Missile carried by an aircraft enabling a target to be attacked without flying directly to it

STEALTH TECHNIQUE
Configuring and coating aircraft so as to reduce reflectivity to radar

STRATEGIC BOMBING
Long-range bombing of a combatant's homeland

STRATEGIC FORCE
That portion of nuclear or conventional missiles and bomber forces devoted to attacking targets in the homeland of an enemy

STRATEGIC WEAPON
A nuclear weapon intended for use against the homeland of an enemy, usually at long range

SUPERCRITICAL MASS
Mass with a density greater than the minimum necessary to sustain a chain reaction

TERMINAL PHASE
Similar to the reentry phase

THIRD WORLD COUNTRIES
The underdeveloped countries, mostly in the southern hemisphere, that are not included in the developed countries

THROW WEIGHT
A ballistic missile's payload capacity, expressed in terms of the RV, its warhead(s) and associated devices, such as arming and fusing systems and penetration aids

TRAJECTORY
Curve described by a projectile as a result of given forces

TWO-KEY WEAPON
Weapon requiring the cooperation of two operators, sometimes of different nationalities, before it can be used

WARSAW PACT
Military alliance of seven Eastern European countries in response to the creation of NATO and the remilitarization of West Germany in the 1950s

X-RAYS
Radiation with a wave length about 1,000 times shorter than visible light and capable of penetrating many solid materials

YIELD
The explosive power of a nuclear weapon, expressed as an equivalent in metric tons of TNT

Index